CCSS Genre Fiction

P9-DGB-153

? Essential Question
How can a pet be an important friend?

A New Home for Henry

by Michael McDade

illustrated by Alessia Girasole

I have a pet turtle named Henry.
Dad bought him for me. Henry and
I are best friends. We have so much
fun together.

Henry lives in a tank in my room. He keeps me company. He always listens to what I say. We have a good relationship. He likes it when I scratch his head.

I like to watch him swim in the tank.
He also enjoys lying on his rock.

"Henry sleeps a lot," says Dad.

"Yes, turtles like to sleep," I say.

Henry eats all kinds of things. He eats fruit and vegetables. He also eats turtle food from the pet store. But Henry likes worms best of all.

Dad brings him worms from the garden to eat.

"Look, Sara, I found Henry some dinner," he says.

Lately, Henry has changed. He doesn't look happy. He has lost his appetite. He just sits and stares.

"He's not even eating worms," says Dad. "I'm worried."

"Is Henry sick?" I ask Dad.

"I don't know, Sara," Dad says. "Let's take him to the pet store."

The next day, Dad and I take Henry to the pet store. We talk to the owner about Henry.

"Turtles like to live outside," she says. "You need to move Henry into your yard."

"Turtles need space to move around," the owner says. "They need some sun as well as some shade."

She shows us a turtle in a large pen. The turtle is hiding there behind some plants. I glance at Dad. He smiles at me.

"Yes, Sara, we can build a proper pen for Henry," he says. "We'll build it in the yard. It will be a nice place for him to live. We'll make it safe for him."

I'm sad that Henry can't stay in my room, but I want him to have lots of space. His friendship is important to me and I want him to be happy.

The next day, Dad and I decide where to build Henry's pen.

"This is a great spot," I say. "It's sunny all morning. It also has some leafy plants for shade."

"You're right, Sara," says Dad. "Let's build it here."

Henry is good at digging. He also loves exploring. Sometimes he tries to climb out of his tank. We make walls out of wood to keep Henry in the pen. Then we dig a shallow trench around the bottom of the walls. We put bricks in the trench. This will keep him from digging under the walls. I would worry about him if he got lost.

Henry likes hiding under different things, so we put two small logs in the pen. I put in a wooden box for Henry's house.

"Turtles also like to lie on rocks to warm themselves," says Dad.

We trade some of the small rocks for a larger rock. It will also make shade for Henry on hot days.

When I glance in the pen, I notice something is missing.

"Henry needs water," I say. "He needs water to swim in."

We have a small tub from the pet store. We dig a hole and put the tub in. Henry will be able to climb in and out easily.

Then we put Henry in his new home. The first thing he does is climb into the tub.

"Look at him splash," says Dad. "He loves his new home."

I'll miss having Henry in my room. But he's happy in his pen. And that makes me happy too.

Respond to Reading

Summarize

Use important details to summarize *A New Home for Henry*.

Character	Setting	Events

Text Evidence

1. How do you know *A New Home for Henry* is fiction? Genre

2. How does Sara feel about Henry? Use details from the illustrations to support your answer. Use Illustrations

3. What is the meaning of *trench* on page 12? Sentence clues will help. Sentence Clues

4. Write about Sara's relationship with Henry. Illustrations will help. Write About Reading

Compare Texts
Read about another pet who is an important friend.

My Best Friend Forever

My best friend forever
Is a green frog named Trevor.

On a leash made of string,
He does his own thing.

When he hops down the street,
All the people we meet

Stop, point, and stare.
They think it's quite rare,

For a frog on the street
To hop over their feet.

But I never will trade
The friend that I've made.

He says, "Give me a squeeze,
Not too hard, if you please."

Three cheers for old Trevor,
My best friend forever!

Make Connections

How are Henry and Trevor important friends? **Essential Question**

How are the feelings of the pet owners in the story and the poem alike? **Text to Text**

Focus on
Literary Elements

Rhyme Words that rhyme have the same ending sound.

What to Look For In "My Best Friend Forever," the words *string* and *thing* have the same ending sound. Find other words in the poem that rhyme. Which of these rhyming words have endings that are spelled the same? Which of these words have endings that are spelled differently?

Your Turn

Write a poem about an animal that is your friend. Can you use words that rhyme at the ends of the lines?